Hot and Cold Sandwiches

Hot and Cold Sandwiches

CAROL BOWEN

SHOOTING STAR PRESS

This edition printed in 1995 for:
Shooting Star Press Inc
230 Fifth Avenue – Suite 1212
New York, NY 10001

Shooting Star Press books are available at special discounts for bulk purchases for sales promotions,
premiums, fund-raising, or educational use. Special edition or book excerpts can also be created to
specification. For details contact: Special Sales Director, Shooting Star Press Inc.,
230 Fifth Avenue, Suite 1212, New York, NY 10001

© Parragon Book Service Ltd 1994

ISBN 1 56924 229 1

Printed in Italy

Acknowledgements:

Design & DTP: Pedro & Frances Prá-Lopez / Kingfisher Design
Art Direction: Lisa Tai
Editor: Linda Doeser Publishing Services
Special Photography: Amanda Heywood
Home Economist: Nicola Fowler
Stylist: Marian Price

Gas Hob supplied by New World Domestic Appliances Ltd
Photographs on pages 6, 20, 34, 48, 62: Tony Stone Images

Contents

Hot Sandwiches

Broiled, toasted, baked or fried, hot sandwiches are equally ideal for the solitary diner or football club. However, to be enjoyed at their best they should be eaten the moment they emerge from the pan, toaster or oven.

This may be a problem when catering for large numbers. Have your broiled, toasted and 'filled for the oven' sandwich combinations prepared well ahead, perhaps in the freezer or the refrigerator ready for cooking. There is no need to thaw frozen sandwiches for toasting or broiling – they become particularly light and crispy when toasted straight from the freezer. Enlist the aid of a helper – this is definitely a two-person operation!

Fried sandwiches, such as the classic Croque Monsieur, are lusciously rich and make a warming snack or appetizing lunch or supper dish. They need to be cooked quickly so timing is crucial. This ensures that the filling will melt, as the bread becomes crisp and golden brown. For best results, fry in a mixture of butter and oil; the butter adds flavor while the oil enables a high enough temperature to be reached for crisp results. Drain on paper towels and serve while still piping hot!

Opposite: *There are numerous varieties of bread that are ideal for hot sandwich fillings.*

STEP 2

STEP 3

STEP 5

STEP 6

ITALIAN HEROES

These are long, crusty rolls that are split in half lengthwise, and topped with an onion and green pepper mixture, then covered with hot Italian sausages.

SERVES 4

12 Italian sausages
4 tbsp water
2 tbsp olive or vegetable oil
2 onions, sliced
4 or 5 red or green bell peppers, or a mixture
of both, cored, seeded and cut into strips
4 long, crusty hero-type rolls

1 Put the sausages in a pan with the water. Cover and simmer gently for about 5 minutes. Remove the lid and continue to cook for about 15 minutes, or until the sausages are browned, turning them occasionally.

2 Meanwhile, heat the oil in another pan and sauté the sliced onions for about 5–8 minutes until they are soft but not colored.

3 Add the pepper strips and continue cooking, stirring occasionally, for about 10 minutes, or until the peppers are tender.

4 Add the sausages and cook for a further 3 minutes.

5 Split the rolls in half lengthwise. Spoon some of the cooked pepper

and onion mixture onto the bottom half of each roll.

6 Top each roll bottom with three of the sausages, then replace the top half of each roll. Cut each roll in half crosswise to serve.

ITALIAN SAUSAGES

Choose from meaty frying sausages such as *luganega*, spicy pork sausages from Romagna in the north (*salsiccia al metro*), which are sold in lengths; or *salamelle*, small, spicy sausages linked in a chain. Although the Italians would make these rolls spicy by using hot sausages, you may like to use plain sausages then spice up the onion mixture by adding 1-2 tbsp sun-dried or plain tomato paste mixed with a generous pinch of chili powder or a dash of chili sauce.

STEP 1

STEP 2

STEP 4

STEP 6

CROQUE MONSIEUR

This classic French sandwich is usually fried in butter and oil.
Here is a neater way to cook it – in the oven.

SERVES 4

8 thick slices white bread, crusts removed
mustard, to taste
4 oz Gruyère cheese, sliced
4 oz cooked ham, thinly sliced
3 tbsp butter, melted

1 Heat the oven to 450°F. Spread half of the slices of white bread with mustard to taste. (Dijon mustard is the traditional choice, but you may prefer to use a hotter mustard, or one of the many herbed mustard varieties that are now widely available.)

2 Trim the cheese slices to fit and put them on the bread. Trim the ham slices to fit and place them on top of the cheese.

3 Top with the remaining slices of bread to make sandwiches, and place them on a baking sheet.

4 Brush the sandwiches lightly with some of the melted butter, setting the remaining butter aside.

5 Cook in the top of the oven for about 5 minutes, or until lightly browned. Turn the sandwiches over with a spatula, brush with the remaining butter and cook for a further 3–5 minutes.

6 Cut the sandwiches in half and serve them hot, wrapped in small paper napkins. Garnish with salad leaves if desired.

ADAPTING CROQUE MONSIEUR

Whole-wheat or mixed-grain bread can be used instead of white bread to create Croque Monsieur, if you prefer. You may even like to add tomato slices.

If you prefer to fry these sandwiches do so in ¼ cup butter with 2 tsp olive or corn oil until golden brown on both sides – about 1-2 minutes. Drain well on paper towels before halving to serve as above.

PO'-BOY SANDWICH

Generally battered and deep-fried, here the oysters are simply broiled and served with a garlic and herb dressing.

STEP 1

STEP 2

STEP 3

STEP 4

SERVES 4

16 fresh oysters
3 tbsp olive oil
2 tbsp sweet butter
1 clove garlic, crushed
1 tbsp chopped fresh parsley
freshly ground black pepper
1 tsp lemon juice
4 slices bacon
2 baguettes
Hot-pepper sauce

1 Broil the oysters, flat shells uppermost, until the shells open slightly. The oyster liquid will start to bubble out of the shells after about 3–5 minutes. Hold the oysters in a cloth, insert a knife between the shells and twist off the top shell. Slip the knife under the oyster to release it from the bottom shell. Put the oysters in a bowl with their juices.

2 Stretch the bacon with the back of a knife, then cut each slice into 4 pieces and make 4 small bacon rolls from each.

3 Heat the oil and butter with the garlic in a small pan. Add the parsley, black pepper to taste and lemon juice, mixing well.

4 Thread the oysters and bacon rolls onto 4 lightly oiled skewers. Brush with the buttery sauce and broil for 2 minutes on each side, basting frquently until cooked.

5 Halve each baguette lengthwise, and toast the cut sides until golden. Drizzle with the remaining garlic oil mixture.

6 Remove the oysters and bacon from the skewers and arrange on the bread. Sprinkle a little hot-pepper sauce on top and serve at once.

A SOUTHERN CLASSIC

This is the famous Louisiana sandwich, packed with any number of fillings, from the more-usual ham, cheese and turkey to soft-shelled crab and oysters. So experiment with your favorite fillings.

STEP 1

STEP 2

STEP 4

STEP 5

FRIED REUBEN SANDWICH

These sandwiches are made of rye bread, stuffed fit to burst with corned beef and sauerkraut, and fried until crisp and golden. They satisfy even man-sized appetites!

SERVES 4

6 tbsp mayonnaise
1 tbsp finely chopped green bell pepper
1 tbsp mild chili sauce
8 slices rye bread
1 cup canned or bottled sauerkraut
3 oz Gruyère or Swiss cheese
8 oz corned beef, sliced
¼ cup butter or margarine
1 tbsp oil

1 Mix the mayonnaise with the chopped green pepper and chili sauce, blending together well.

2 Spread about 1 tablespoon of the pepper mixture onto each slice of rye bread.

3 Drain the sauerkraut and slice the cheese into 8 pieces.

4 Place a piece of cheese (sliced quite thickly) on four slices of the bread. Top each slice with a quarter of the corned beef and a quarter of the sauerkraut. Cover each with another slice of cheese, then sandwich together with the remaining slices of bread, mayonnaise sides down.

5 Melt the butter or margarine and oil in a large, heavy-based skillet. Add the sandwiches one by one and cook on one side for about 3–4 minutes until golden. Turn over and cook for a further 3–4 minutes until crisp and brown.

6 Drain on paper towels. Cut in half and serve at once, garnished with sliced pickles if desired.

A MILD CHANGE

Not surprisingly, these sandwiches originated in Germany. But chili sauce was not part of the original recipe. If you have a sensitive palate, you may wish to leave out the chili sauce for a milder flavor.

14

ITALIAN MOZZARELLA LOAF

This is a delicious pull-apart type of sandwich that makes a welcome appearance on the cold buffet table or at an outdoor barbecue when the weather turns a little chilly!

STEP 1

SERVES 4–6

1 tsp oil
1 x 1 lb rye and caraway seed loaf, not sliced
8 oz mozzarella cheese
¼ cup butter, softened
10–12 anchovy fillets
12 ripe olives, halved and pitted
½ tsp dried marjoram
1 tsp fresh chopped basil or ½ tsp dried

5 Place the loaf on the greased baking sheet and bake in the oven for 15 minutes until it is crisp and golden brown and the cheese is bubbly.

6 Allow the loaf to stand for a few minutes before serving. Pull the slices of bread apart to eat.

STEP 2

1 Heat the oven to 425°F. Lightly grease a baking sheet with the oil. On a bread board, slice the loaf of bread at 1 in intervals almost through to the base, being careful not to cut it all the way through.

2 Cut the mozzarella into thin slices and insert each slice between the slices of bread.

3 Using a flat-bladed knife, spread the top of the loaf of bread with the softened butter.

4 Place the anchovies over the top of the bread in a crisscross pattern. Scatter the olives on top and sprinkle with the herbs.

STEP 3

MARINATED OLIVES

It is easy to marinate your own olives, for added flavor in this recipe. Drain a jar of ripe olives and place in a clean screwtop jar. Add peeled garlic cloves, orange peel and a sprig of fresh rosemary or thyme. Add olive oil to just cover the olives, cover the jar and leave the olives to marinate for at least a day.

STEP 4

STEP 1

STEP 2

STEP 3

STEP 4

CHEESE SHRIMPY

This is a Danish oven-baked open-faced sandwich that is ideal to serve for a light supper or as a first course to a meal.

SERVES 2

3 oz semihard cheese, such as Samsoe or
    Edam
1 cup shelled cooked shrimp
2 tbsp mayonnaise
1 tbsp sour cream or plain yogurt
juice of $\frac{1}{2}$ lemon
salt and pepper
3 tbsp butter
4 slices close-textured white bread
2 egg whites
parsley sprigs and 4 unshelled shrimp, to
    garnish

1 Heat the oven to 400°F. Grate the cheese and set aside, together with a few shrimp for the garnish.

2 Mix the remaining shrimp with the mayonnaise, sour cream or yogurt and lemon juice. Season to taste.

3 Butter the slices of bread and divide the shrimp mixture between the slices to cover each slice evenly.

4 Beat the egg whites until they stand in stiff peaks. Fold in the grated cheese. Spread the egg and cheese

mixture onto the bread, being sure to completely cover the shrimp and mayonnaise mixture.

5 Place on a baking sheet and cook in the oven for about 20–25 minutes until golden brown.

6 Transfer to a warmed serving plate, garnish with the reserved shrimp and the parsley sprigs and serve while still hot.

LIGHT OPTIONS

If you are keeping an eye on your weight, try substituting low-calorie mayonnaise and lowfat yogurt or sour cream in this recipe. It still tastes sensational, without being too high in fat.

Vegetarian Sandwiches

Whether you need a light lunch for two to break the day, a tray full of hearty nibbles to serve with pre-dinner drinks, or a speedy yet sustaining snack to replace a main meal, a sandwich will fit the bill. Even with the need for a vegetarian option, the range and choice will still be wide. Sometimes a little extra ingenuity is called into play, but that just adds to the excitement and novelty of the combinations possible.

Natural filling ingredients include cheese (and now there are so many vegetarian types available from Cheddar to mozzarella); salad leaves in all their guises from mild corn salad to sharp, pungent radicchio; rich, sweet tomatoes from the minature cherry size to the hand-sized 'beef' (so perfect for slicing thickly); Mediterranean-style vegetables such as bell peppers, onion, zucchini, eggplant and fennel; eggs, hard-boiled and sliced, chopped and made creamy with mayonnaise or scrambled with asparagus, mushrooms or bell peppers; nuts, seeds and sprouts to give a munch and a crunch to a creamy or smooth filling; and grapes, apples, pears, bananas and luscious peaches or nectarines to give a fruity lift.

Choose breads that interest too: nutty and seeded varieties or flavored types made with onion, cheese, olives or herbs. Then stuff to bursting with an imaginative filling from the selection here.

Opposite: *Crispy vegetables and sweet, crunchy fruit make a myriad of delicious vegetarian fillings.*

STEP 1

STEP 3

STEP 4

STEP 5

GREEK FETA SLICE

This is a wonderfully colorful and aromatic hot sandwich idea that makes a good first course or light lunch dish. For authenticity use Greek Halloumi or feta cheese.

SERVES 4

²/₃ cup olive oil
1 large clove garlic, crushed
1 tsp chopped fresh thyme
1 tbsp lemon juice
salt and pepper
1 small eggplant, sliced, and cut into bite-sized pieces
1 large zucchini, thickly sliced
1 small bulb fennel, sliced and cut into bite-sized chunks
1 small red bell pepper, cored, seeded and cut into pieces
1 small yellow bell pepper, cored, seeded and cut into pieces
1 onion, cut into thin wedges
4 large thick slices country-style white crusty bread
4 oz Greek cheese (Halloumi or feta, for example), sliced or broken into pieces
8 ripe olives, pitted and cut into strips

1 Beat the oil with the garlic, thyme, lemon juice and salt and pepper to taste in a large bowl.

2 Add the prepared eggplant, zucchini, fennel, bell peppers and onion, mixing well. Cover and leave to stand for about 1 hour, stirring occasionally.

3 Spread the vegetable mixture on a broiler pan or baking sheet with upturned edges. Cook under a preheated moderate broiler for about 15 minutes, turning over frequently, until the vegetables are tender and lightly charred around the edges. Keep warm.

4 Meanwhile, brush the bread with a little of the cooking juices from the vegetables and toast lightly on both sides until just crisp and golden.

5 Top each slice of bread with the cheese slices or pieces, then cover with a generous amount of the cooked vegetable mixture.

6 Return to the broiler and cook for a further 3–5 minutes or until the cheese is bubbly. Serve at once, garnished with the olive strips.

BUCK RAREBIT

If Welsh Rarebit makes a delicious snack, then Buck Rarebit makes a complete sandwich style meal!

STEP 1

MAKES 6

¼ cup butter
6 tomatoes, halved
3 cups mushrooms, wiped and halved
6 eggs
6 slices of bread
1 cup Cheddar cheese, grated
½ cup fresh Parmesan cheese, grated
salt and pepper
pinch of dry mustard powder
5 tbsp milk

mustard powder and milk, stirring well to make a thick paste.

5 Spread the paste onto the toast. Place the toast slices on a rack under a preheated moderate broiler, and cook until golden and bubbly, about 3-5 minutes.

6 Transfer the slices of toast to warmed serving plates. Top each slice with a poached egg and garnish with the halved tomatoes and mushrooms. Serve at once.

STEP 2

1 Put a knob of butter on each tomato half and each mushroom and cook slowly under a preheated broiler for about 4–5 minutes until cooked. Keep warm.

2 Poach the eggs in gently simmering water until just cooked. Remove from the heat and keep warm.

3 Meanwhile, toast the bread and remove the crusts if preferred. Spread lightly with the remaining butter.

4 Mix the Cheddar with the Parmesan cheese, season to taste with salt and pepper, then add the

STEP 4

FOR GARLIC LOVERS

If you can't resist adding garlic to savory dishes, try making your Buck Rarebit using butter mixed with a clove of crushed garlic. Simply use it instead of plain butter on the tomatoes and mushrooms and when buttering the bread.

STEP 6

STEP 1

STEP 3

STEP 4

STEP 6

SALAD DAYS

When the sun is sizzling high in the sky, a light salad
sandwich is always welcome.

SERVES 1

2 tbsp butter
1 tsp snipped fresh chives
1 tsp lemon juice
4 slices mixed-grain bread
a little shredded crisp lettuce
2 hard-boiled eggs
2 tbsp mayonnaise or plain yogurt
1/2 avocado, seeded
salt and pepper

1 Beat the butter with the chives and half of the lemon juice to make a smooth spread.

2 Spread the slices of bread with the prepared chive butter, then cover two slices with shredded lettuce.

3 Shell and chop the hard-boiled eggs and place in a bowl with the mayonnaise or fromage frais and mix gently to coat.

4 Peel the avocado, cut into chunky slices or bite-sized cubes and toss with the remaining lemon juice to prevent discoloration.

5 Add the avocado to the egg mixture and fold gently to mix.

6 Spoon the mixture onto the shredded lettuce and place the remaining slices of bread on top. Press lightly to seal, then cut into halves or quarters to serve.

VARIATIONS

Avocado adds a creamy texture to this filling, as well as color, but it is loaded with calories. For a lowfat option, replace it with two finely chopped potatoes and use lowfat yogurt instead of mayonnaise. For a crunchy texture, add a very finely chopped celery stalk.

In this recipe, you can make good use of the wide variety of crisp lettuce and salad greens now on the market. Crisp Cos, Webbs or Iceberg lettuce are natural choices but also consider shredded Chinese cabbage; slightly bitter or crisp Radicchio; and wild or red chicory, purslane, dandelion or burnet.

PIZZA TOASTS

Italian ciabatta bread is a floury, rough textured bread that makes the perfect base for a pizza-style sandwich dish.

STEP 2

STEP 3

STEP 4

STEP 5

SERVES 2-4

1 ciabatta loaf or any floury, rough-textured loaf
$^1/_2$ cup sun-dried-tomato and herb spread (see box)
$^2/_3$ cup Cheddar cheese, roughly grated
1 red onion, sliced
8 oz tomatoes, sliced
4 oz mozzarella cheese, sliced quite finely
fresh basil sprigs, to garnish

1 Heat the oven to 425°F. Split the ciabatta loaf in half lengthwise.

2 Spread the sun-dried-tomato and herb paste evenly over both of the cut surfaces of the loaf.

3 Top the sun-dried-tomato and herb paste with the grated Cheddar cheese, followed by the red onion separated into rings, tomatoes, and finally the sliced mozzarella cheese.

4 Place both halves of the loaf on a large baking sheet and cook in the oven for 10–15 minutes, or until it is browned and crisp on top and the cheese is bubbling.

5 Remove from the oven and garnish with the basil sprigs.

6 Cut into thick slices or leave in halves to serve.

QUICK TOPPINGS

The joy of this recipe is that it uses a prepared spread from the supermarket, so it is very quick to prepare. This example uses ready-prepared chopped sun-dried tomatoes with herbs and oil as its base, but this can be replaced with pesto sauce for a more gutsy flavor. You can also use a prepared tomato sauce with garlic and herbs. Look at the delicatessen section of your supermarket for other ideas.

STEP 1

STEP 3

STEP 4

STEP 6

WALNUT FINGER SANDWICH

Even the simplest sandwiches can be given a new twist if you make them with an unusual bread. The recipe filling below goes admirably with a nut bread such as walnut.

SERVES 1

2 tbsp butter or margarine
1 tsp finely grated onion
$\frac{1}{2}$ tsp snipped chives or chopped fresh
   parsley
salt and pepper
4 slices walnut bread
3 oz Roquefort cheese or other blue cheese
about 6 black grapes
sprigs of parsley or watercress, to garnish,
   if liked

1 Beat the butter with the grated onion and parsley or chives to make a smooth spread. Season to taste with salt and pepper.

2 Spread the slices of bread with the prepared butter.

3 Slice the Roquefort cheese thinly and layer the cheese onto two of the slices of bread so that the pieces of cheese overlap slightly.

4 Halve the grapes and remove any seeds. Place on top of the cheese slices, cut sides down.

5 Cover with the remaining slices of bread and press gently to seal.

6 Cut into thick finger sandwiches to serve. Garnish with parsley or watercress, if liked.

A blue cheese is the best companion for the nutty bread and grapes in this recipe. If you do not like blue cheese, replace it with a hard cheese with a sharp flavor.

NEW BREADS

Supermarket shelves and bakeries boast imaginative varieties of bread, from simple onion, nut and seeded to special olive and sun-dried-tomato studded types.

VEGETARIAN MUNCH AND CRUNCH

Vegetarian lunch boxes needn't resemble rabbit-food boxes if a selection of fruit, vegetables and dairy products is mixed imaginatively. The recipe below produces a sandwich with lots of munch and crunch!

STEP 1

MAKES **2**

3 tbsp smooth peanut butter
¼ cup cream cheese
1 small carrot
1 celery stalk
4 green olives
small handful of alfalfa sprouts or bean
    sprouts
½ small red apple
2 tsp lemon juice
2 large whole-wheat rolls or buns

1 In a small bowl mix the peanut butter with the cream cheese to make a smooth spread.

2 Grate the carrot, finely chop the celery and dice the olives. Add to the spread and, using a wooden spoon, mix gently but thoroughly to combine.

3 Place the alfalfa sprouts or beansprouts in another bowl. Core but do not peel the apple, then dice. Add to the sprouts with the lemon juice and toss well to mix.

4 Cut the rolls or baps (buns) in half and spread each half generously with the vegetable, peanut butter and cream cheese mixture.

5 Top each roll with half of the sprout-and-apple mixture, replace the lids and press gently to seal.

6 Wrap in foil to transport in a lunch box if required.

STEP 2

STEP 3

ALTERNATIVES

For a change, replace butter with other spreads, such as mayonnaise, sandwich spreads, savory pastes or spreads, bouillon-based spreads or well-seasoned vegetable purées.

Any number of different fruits can be used in this sandwich filling to produce a delicious variation on a theme. Consider adding diced pear, snipped dried apricot, diced fresh peach or nectarine, chopped fresh apricot or chopped banana to the sprout mixture instead of diced apple.

STEP 5

33

Big & Filling Sandwiches

It is generally recognized that the sandwich is universal and that every country, even every region, seems to have its own sandwich creation. It is hardly surprising, since the early origins of sandwich fare lie in the roots of peasant food. They may differ appreciably in their contents but all have one underlying theme – they are big, hearty, filling and generously-filled.
Most, such as the French Pan Bagnat, the Swedish Landganger (an open sandwich made on the spot by Swedish farm laborers), the Club Sandwich and the Irish Bookmaker's Sandwich, use local and inexpensive ingredients and follow fairly specific guidelines on preparation.
Many of these are the sandwiches to prepare to replace a main meal dish. Hearty sandwiches don't necessarily mean door-stop-sized wedges of bread, although some are sliced generously, but the fillings are always on the heavy side. Many are better served with a knife and fork although that can destroy the spirit of the informal meal. These are also the sandwiches to take on picnics – fresh air definitely sharpens appetites.

Opposite: *Hearty sandwiches made from a range of delicious breads provide a mouthwatering alternative to a main meal dish.*

NICOISE SANDWICH

This is a rough country-style sandwich particularly well known in the South of France in the Provence or Côte d'Azur region.

STEP 1

STEP 3

STEP 4

STEP 5

SERVES 2

1 country-style loaf, ideally round, about
    7 inches in diameter
1 clove garlic, cut in half
5 tbsp olive oil
4 firm tomatoes, sliced
1/2 green bell pepper, cored and sliced
2 oz canned anchovy fillets, drained
1/2 cup canned tuna, drained and flaked
4 ripe or green olives, pitted
2 tsp capers, well drained
salt and pepper
1 tbsp lemon juice or wine vinegar

1 Cut the bread in half horizontally and rub the cut surfaces with the clove of garlic.

2 Sprinkle about 3 tablespoons of the olive oil over each bread half, drizzling it lightly but evenly over the surfaces.

3 Top the base with the sliced tomatoes. Arrange the pepper slices, anchovy fillets, tuna, olives and capers on top, then season to taste with salt and pepper.

4 Beat the remaining oil with the lemon juice or vinegar to make a dressing and sprinkle it over the top of the sandwich filling.

5 Place the remaining bread half on top of the filling and press down lightly so that the juices mix.

6 Leave to stand for 30 minutes before slicing to serve.

ORIGINS OF THE NICOISE

The niçoise sandwich is derived from the days when peasants simply soaked their bread in olive oil and vinegar and filled it with an assortment of salad ingredients not unlike Salade Niçoise. This "sandwich of the people" is also known as Pan Bagnat.

BOOKMAKER'S SANDWICH

This is a mammoth sandwich of cold steak and mustard in a soft white loaf. It is called this because in Ireland bookmakers would take it to the races for a good satisfying lunch.

STEP 1

SERVES 4

1 long crusty loaf with a soft white crumb
1/2 cup butter
1 1/2 lb filet mignon or sirloin steak, cut
    1 in thick
salt and pepper
1/4 cup horseradish-flavored mustard (or see
    boxed note below for alternatives)
small sprigs of watercress, to garnish
    (optional)

cold. (By wrapping the loaf, you will ensure that the meat doesn't dry out.)

6 Slice the sandwiched loaf into wedges for serving, garnished with watercress sprigs, if liked.

STEP 4

1 Slice the loaf in half lengthwise and butter it thickly.

2 Broil the steaks under a very hot broiler for 2–3 minutes on each side, according to whether you would prefer your steaks to be rare, medium or well-done.

3 Place the hot steaks on one half of the loaf. Sprinkle with salt and pepper to taste.

4 Spread the mustard over the meat, then top with the remaining loaf half. Press down lightly to seal the sandwich and enclose the meat.

5 Wrap the loaf in foil, then set it aside until the meat is completely

HERB AND PEPPER ALTERNATIVES

Although horseradish is the classic flavoring for the mustard used with this sandwich, you might like to experiment with other tastes: there are also prepared mustards available that are flavored with thyme, tarragon and other herbs.

For a steak sandwich with extra kick, prepare the steak *au poivre* before broiling. About one hour before broiling, press 2 tbsp crushed black peppercorns (use a rolling pin for crushing) well into the steaks with the palm of your hand. Leave in a cool place until ready to cook.

STEP 5

STEP 6

STEP 1

STEP 3

STEP 4

STEP 5

PICNIC SANDWICH

This loaf is cooked complete with its filling of flavorful sausage meat, ham and hard-boiled eggs. It is perfect to pack and take along on a picnic, because it will not need any extra attention.

SERVES 8

1 small uncut Italian loaf
6 tbsp butter, melted
1 cup pork sausage meat
1/2 cup cooked ham, diced
1 small onion, finely chopped
2 eggs
2/3 cup milk
2 hard-boiled eggs, shelled and halved
salt and pepper

1 Heat the oven to 400°F. Cut horizontally across the loaf, two-thirds of the way up. and remove the "lid." Gently ease away the bread from around the edge of the crust. Make 2 cups bread crumbs from the bread.

2 Brush the cavity of the loaf and the lid with some of the melted butter.

3 Combine the sausage meat with the diced ham, bread crumbs and onion, mixing together well. Beat the eggs and milk together and stir into the meat mixture.

4 Place one-third of the filling in the bread case and arrange the halved hard-boiled eggs on top. Season to taste with salt and pepper. Pack the bread case with the remaining filling, then top with the bread lid.

5 Secure the loaf in a package like fashion with string. Use the remaining butter to brush all over the loaf. Place on a baking sheet and cook in the oven for 15 minutes.

6 Cover the entire loaf with foil and continue to cook for a further 45 minutes. Remove and allow to cool. When cool, remove the string and cut into thick slices to serve. If you are packing this sandwich for a picnic, leave it unsliced and slice it on the spot.

MEAT MAGIC

This sandwich idea has endless variations if you use flavored sausagemeat to ring the changes in the basic recipe. Some enterprising butchers now offer varieties such as apple and pork, beef and tomato, pork and leek and variations of spiced and plain ingredients.

STEP 2

STEP 3

STEP 4

STEP 6

SAVORY CHEESE FLUFFS

A variation on melted cheese on toast. This is made lighter and fluffier with the addition of egg whites. It makes a most comforting light meal when you want something hot that is quick and easy to make.

MAKES 2

2 slices of bread, toasted
1 tbsp butter or margarine
1/2 cup Cheddar cheese, grated
2-3 tbsp heavy cream
1/4 tsp mustard
1 tbsp snipped fresh chives
salt and pepper
1 egg white
sprigs of parsley and tomato wedges, to
    garnish (optional)

1 Spread the slices of toast with the butter or margarine, spread thinly.

2 Mix the cheese with the cream, mustard, snipped chives and salt and pepper to taste.

3 Beat the egg white until it stands in stiff peaks, then fold into the cheese mixture with a metal spoon.

4 Pile the mixture evenly over the prepared slices of toast.

5 Cook under a preheated low to medium broiler until the topping is golden and fluffy.

6 Serve at once, garnished with parsley sprigs and tomato wedges, if you like.

Like many hot sandwiches, this one is best eaten immediately; it quickly goes limp and the cheese filling will lose its fluffiness if left.

VARIATIONS

Cheddar cheese is always a popular choice for any hot sandwich, but it isn't the only cheese you can use. Freshly grated Parmesan cheese will give a sharp, slightly salty flavor, while Monterey Jack will be much milder tasting. This is a good way to experiment with cheeses you might not have had before. If you buy cheese from the delicatessen counter of your supermarket or from a specialist store, you can ask for a taste before you decide.

BROILED PITA POCKETS

Pita bread is a delicious flat bread that is found thoughout the Middle East. It seems to have been made for stuffing!

STEP 1

STEP 2

STEP 3

STEP 4

SERVES 2

2 pita breads
2 generous handfuls of mixed salad leaves
   (such as mâche, frisée, arugala, chicory
   and radicchio)
2-inch piece cucumber
2 tomatoes
2 scallions
2 tbsp oil-and-vinegar salad dressing
1/2 cup cooked cubed lamb (optional)
1 tsp chopped fresh mint (optional)
3/4 cup cheese, grated

1 Carefully cut an opening into the center of each pita bread but not through to the base. Open out the bread pockets by gently pulling the bread apart.

2 Wash and tear the salad leaves into small pieces. Slice the cucumber, tomatoes and scallions. Mix the salad ingredients together and toss with the prepared dressing. Add the lamb and mint, if using, and mix well.

3 Stuff the bread pockets with the salad mixture.

4 Sprinkle with the cheese so that the salad mixture is covered.

5 Cook under a preheated medium broiler until the cheese is golden and bubbly, about 5–6 minutes.

6 Transfer to plates and serve at once while still hot. Serve with a tomato and onion salad.

FILLING OPTIONS

Lamb is the natural choice for this sandwich because it is such a popular meat in Greece, Turkey and throughout the Middle East, where pita bread is eaten several times a day. But feel free to make this filling with other meat. This is an excellent way to make the most of leftover roast beef or chicken. It would also be good with cold roast pork.

To make your own yogurt salad dressing, beat 2/3 cup plain yogurt with 1 tbsp lemon juice, 1 tsp clear honey, 1/4 tsp mustard and salt and pepper to taste, until smooth and creamy. Flavor with chopped herbs, if liked.

STEP 2

STEP 4

STEP 5

STEP 6

SUPER CLUB SANDWICH

Club sandwiches are intended to be more or less adequate substitutes for a full meal and can be as many layers high as you can manage!

SERVES 1

3 slices white or whole-wheat bread
1/4 cup butter
1 cup crabmeat, flaked and well drained if canned
3 tbsp lemon mayonnaise
salt and pepper
4 small crisp lettuce leaves
1 tomato, sliced
2-inch piece cucumber, sliced
lemon wedges and watercress sprigs, to garnish

1 Toast the slices of bread until golden, then spread each slice with butter.

2 In a small bowl, mix the crabmeat with the mayonnaise and salt and pepper to taste.

3 Cover the first slice of toast with 2 of the lettuce leaves, then half of the crab mixture and the tomato slices.

4 Cover with the second slice of toast, then the remaining crab mayonnaise and the sliced cucumber.

5 Place the third slice of toast on top, buttered side down, and press gently to seal.

6 Cut the whole sandwich into quarters or two large triangles, then secure each with toothpicks. Serve garnished with watercress sprigs and lemon wedge.

SANDWICH HISTORY

Legend has it that a man came home late and hungry from his club one night, raided the refrigerator and made himself a super sandwich, which he dubbed "club". Another says that the chef of a club made himself a reputation by devising a special sandwich. Either way, the club sandwich is now known as the king of sandwiches.

46

Sandwiches for Entertaining

Everyone can recall the party when the canapés were too soggy or too dry yet few can recall super buffet sandwiches that were a joy to eat. Armed with the recipes in this section and a few useful tips you can stand unrivaled as the best party giver around.

If you need to make these sandwiches well ahead of a function, choose bases such as crisp toast or crispy baked bread. Top with a smear of butter to protect the base from moist fillings and toppings. Cover with plastic wrap or foil to prevent drying out. Remember not to stack strong-flavored fillings such as tuna and onion next to mild-flavored fillings as they will absorb the flavor.

Danish Open Faced Sandwiches are ideal to serve at a party as a varied selection can be prepared. The Scandinavians add interest by varying their bread from Danish to rye and whole-wheat – many also use Scandinavian crispbread too. As a general guide, softer breads go better with firm toppings, for example tuna, salmon and salami, and harder breads go better with soft toppings such as cheese or eggs.

Sandwiches can also make a welcome entrance to the smart dinner party set. What could be more enticing at a lazy Sunday brunch than bagels filled with smoked salmon, cream cheese and capers? Toasted goats' cheese on sourdough country-style bread with a designer salad and aromatic salad dressing makes a sophisticated starter to the chicest of dinner party meals.

Opposite: *Sandwiches are ideal for easy entertaining. Countless ingredients can be used in endless combinations.*

STEP 1

STEP 2

STEP 3

STEP 4

PINWHEELS

These pinwheel sandwiches, filled with a bacon and tomato mixture and baked until golden, make delicious nibbles to serve with drinks. They are irresistable served warm or cool.

MAKES 24

8 slices bacon
2 tsp oil
$\frac{1}{2}$ small onion, finely chopped
1 tbsp tomato paste
1 tsp Worcestershire sauce
4 slices of white or whole-wheat bread
1 tbsp butter, melted

1 Heat the oven to 375°F. Lightly grease a large baking sheet. Chop the bacon very finely. Heat the oil in a pan, add the onion and bacon and fry together gently until cooked and turning golden but not brown, as it will be cooked further in the oven.

2 Remove the pan from the heat, then stir in the tomato paste and Worcestershire sauce.

3 Trim the crusts from the bread, then flatten each slice very lightly with a rolling pin.

4 Spread the slices of bread with the prepared filling. Roll up each slice widthwise like a jelly roll, then cut each roll into $\frac{1}{2}$-inch pieces. Secure with toothpicks. Place on the baking sheet and brush with the melted butter.

5 Bake in the oven for 10-12 minutes or until golden brown. Remove the pinwheels from the oven and leave to stand on the sheet for 5 minutes until firm and set.

6 Transfer to a wire rack to cool further. Serve warm or cool.

FINISHING TOUCHES

Add a touch of elegance to a dish of pinwheels with garnishes. Little bouquets of watercress can be made by trimming the ends of a small bunch fairly short. Arrange these around the edges of a plate to give it a fresh and inviting appearance.

STEP 1

STEP 3

STEP 5

STEP 6

HARLEQUIN BUFFET SANDWICH

These sandwiches look so elegant on a formal buffet table. Made from whole-wheat and white breads, they are sandwiched together with three different fillings and then cut to give a harlequin effect.

MAKES 18

8 hard-boiled eggs
1 cup butter or margarine, softened
2 tbsp mayonnaise
salt and pepper
$^{1}/_{3}$ cup shelled cooked shrimp
juice of $^{1}/_{2}$ lemon
2 tsp tomato paste
1 tsp Worcestershire sauce
2 oz liver pâté
6 slices whole-wheat bread
6 slices white bread

1 Shell the eggs and separate the yolks from the whites. Sieve the egg yolks and, separately, chop the whites very finely.

2 In a bowl, cream together ¼ cup of the butter with the egg yolks, mayonnaise and salt and pepper to taste. Divide the mixture into 3 portions.

3 Finely chop the shrimp, add the lemon juice and half the chopped egg white and mix with one-third of the creamed egg mixture. Save the remaining egg whites and use them later in another recipe, or discard them if they won't be needed.

4 Stir the tomato paste and Worcestershire sauce into another third of the creamed egg, butter and mayonnaise mixture.

5 Mash the liver pâté and blend with the remaining one-third of the egg mixture. Butter the sliced white and whole-wheat bread. Using alternate layers of whole-wheat and white bread, sandwich together with the three fillings using four slices of bread per sandwich. Press well together, wrap in foil and chill until required.

6 Remove the crusts from the sandwiches and cut into ¼-in slices. Arrange on a plate to serve.

52

STEP 1 (BLUE BOY)

STEP 2 (BLUE BOY)

STEP 1 (COPENHAGEN)

STEP 2 (TIVOLI)

DANISH OPEN-FACED TRIO

*The Danish gentry originally were served their meat on slices of bread.
The meat was eaten but the bread was not – it was given to the servants.
Perhaps this is the origin of the Danish open-faced sandwich.*

MAKES 3

*For all sandwiches use 3 slices of close-
textured bread, spread with butter or
margarine. You can also use rye or
pumpernickle bread.*

BLUE BOY

*1 small lettuce leaf (such as iceberg or
  Boston lettuce)
3 slices blue brie cheese
3 seedless black grape halves*

1 To make the Blue Boy sandwich,
place the lettuce leaf at one end of a
slice of bread. Arrange the slices of cheese
on the bread so that they overlap.

2 Garnish each slice of the blue
cheese with a black grape half.

COPENHAGEN

*1 thin slice roast beef
1 small lettuce leaf
2 tsp mayonnaise
1 tsp fried onions
1 tsp grated horseradish
1 pickle fan
1 slice tomato*

1 To make the Copenhagen open-
faced sandwich, arrange the beef
slice to cover one slice of bread. Place the
lettuce leaf at one end of the sandwich
and spoon on the mayonnaise to hold
down but not cover the lettuce leaf. Add a
scattering of onion and horseradish.

2 Position the pickle fan opposite the
lettuce leaf and top the entire
sandwich with a tomato twist.

TIVOLI

*1 large lettuce leaf
4 slices hard-boiled egg
4 slices tomato
1–2 tbsp mayonnaise
1/2 tbsp Danish-style caviare or lumpfish roe*

1 To make the Tivoli open-faced
sandwich, cover the final slice of
bread with the lettuce leaf. Arrange the
egg and tomato slices in two rows
lengthwise on the lettuce.

2 Pipe or spoon the mayonnaise
down the center of the egg and
tomato slices, and spoon the caviare over
the mayonnaise.

COUNTRY CROUTE

This is one of the simplest yet most sophisticated baked sandwiches – good enough to serve as first course at a dinner party. Remember, however, to use the very best bread, chèvre cheese, oil and salad leaves.

STEP 1

STEP 2

SERVES 4

4 thin slices of country-style French bread
   (sourdough, for example)
4 small goat cheeses or 1 x 4 oz chèvre log,
   sliced into 4 portions
2–3 tbsp olive or hazelnut oil
1 clove garlic, crushed (optional)
mixed salad leaves to serve (mâche, frisée,
   arugala, chicory and radicchio for
   example)
4 tbsp oil-and-vinegar dressing with herbs
   (either a good quality prepared dressing or
   your own blend)

1 Heat the oven to 400°F. Place the slices of bread on a lightly greased baking sheet and top each with a whole small goat cheese or thick slice of chèvre log.

2 Mix the oil with the crushed garlic, if used, then drizzle over the cheese and bread.

3 Bake in the oven for about 10–15 minutes, or until the cheese bubbles and browns on top.

4 Meanwhile, toss the salad leaves in the dressing and divide between four individual serving plates.

5 Top each serving of salad with a freshly baked *croûte* and serve while still warm.

A supply of *croûtes* can be kept in reserve in the freezer for later use. Drain the fried *croûtes* on paper towels and then pack them, interleaved with waxed paper, in a double layer of freezer wrap. Warm thoroughly when needed.

STEP 4

THE CROUTE FAMILY

Bread cut into various shapes can be used as a base for serving food – *croûtes* – or as a decoration – croutons. *Croûtes* can be used as a base on which to serve small game birds or noisettes of meat.

STEP 5

STEP 1

STEP 2

STEP 4

STEP 5

NEW YORK BAGELS

When a special Sunday brunch or lazy, late breakfast is on the cards, nothing, simply nothing, is better than this cream cheese and smoked salmon bagel.

SERVES 2

4 plain or onion bagels
1 tbsp butter (optional)
$^1/_2$ cup cream cheese
1 tsp grated lemon rind
1 tbsp capers, well drained
a little shredded crisp lettuce (iceberg is best for this)
4 oz smoked salmon

Slice the bagels in half and spread with a little butter, if liked.

1 Mix the cream cheese with the grated lemon rind, beating well until the mixture becomes smooth and creamy. Finely chop 1 teaspoon of the capers and add to the cheese mixture, mixing well to blend.

2 Divide the cream cheese mixture equally between the bagels, spreading evenly.

3 Cover the cream cheese mixture with a little shredded lettuce.

4 Cut the smoked salmon into thick strips and divide between the bagels evenly. Scatter the remaining capers on top.

5 Replace the bagel tops and press down on them gently to seal. Serve as soon as possible.

BAGELS AND SALMON

Bagels come in all guises – plain, sprinkled and flavored with onion seeds, speckled with caraway seeds, and even studded with raisins and flavored with cinnamon. Plain or flavored varieties are also delicious with cream cheese alone.

Other cured or smoked fish can be used instead of smoked salmon in this recipe. Try using smoked eel, gravad lax (cured salmon with a dill coating), smoked sturgeon or smoked halibut. Thinly slice and cut into strips before adding to the bagels. Gravad lax strips can be topped with a mustardy dill sauce instead of capers, if you prefer.

STEP 1

STEP 3

STEP 4

STEP 5

CITY TOASTS

This is an old Victorian sandwich recipe that will prove just as delicious and popular today.

SERVES 6

½ cup butter, softened
½ cup Gruyère cheese, grated
½ cup fresh Parmesan cheese, grated
2 tsp heavy cream
salt and cayenne pepper
6 x 3½-inch slices of white or whole-wheat
    bread
3 slices garlic, ham or liver sausage, halved
3 slices Gruyère cheese, halved
6 gherkins, to garnish

1 In a bowl, blend the butter together with the grated Gruyère cheese, Parmesan cheese and cream, using a wooden spoon. Season the mixture to taste with salt and cayenne pepper.

2 Lightly toast the bread until golden and crisp.

3 Divide the cheese mixture equally between the pieces of toast, spreading lightly to cover.

4 Place a halved slice of sausage and cheese on top of the filling on each slice of toast, setting them at an angle so that they look like "wings".

5 Slice the gherkins to make fans, cutting each one several times along its length without cutting through fully at the end. Garnish each toast with a gherkin, and serve.

A COFFEE HOUSE FAVORITE

The name of these toasts derives from a London tradition. Platters of City Toasts were served at some of the most famous City of London coffeehouses in the 19th century while the gentlemen guests played chess.

Create variety by varying the garnish on these sandwiches. Instead of decorating with gherkin fans, try scallion curls, cucumber twists, carrot curls, sliced olives, small tomato roses or herb bows and bundles.

Kids' Sandwiches

For lots of reasons – price, availability, choice and convenience – more children than ever are taking packed lunches to school every day. If your child takes a regular lunch box then remember to choose sandwiches that include as many of the basic food groups as possible, incorporating protein in the form of eggs, cheese, meat, fish, poultry or legumes; carbohydrate in the bread itself; fat in the form of butter, margarine or a dressing; and vitamins, minerals and fiber in vegetables, fruit and whole-wheat breads. The recipe for Cheese and Apple Delights fits the bill admirably. Serve together with a glass or carton of milk or fruit juice and a piece of fresh fruit for a superbly well-balanced meal.

Kid's party fare is quite a different matter – the savory sandwich selection must be appealing, especially if it has to entice children away from the sweeter offerings, but nutrition doesn't play such a vital role with such once-in-a-while treats. The emphasis here is on fun, attractiveness and variety. And what could be more attractive than an armada of egg filled boats set on a sea green layer of salad leaves or fishy slices of toast topped with letters to represent the names of the party guests (this also takes the guesswork out of who has eaten and who has not)! Fussy eaters will be enchanted with a game board pizza made with edible noughts and crosses on a crispy bread slice where everyone is a winner.

Opposite: *Fussy eaters will always be tempted by delicious breads of all shapes and sizes.*

STEP 1

STEP 3

STEP 4

STEP 5

HOT DIGGITTY DOGS

Diggitty dogs are hot-dog buns spread with mustard and filled with a chili-onion garnish, then topped with frankfurters. They make wonderful barbecue fare – popular with children and adults alike.

SERVES 8

8 hot-dog buns
8 tsp mild (or a hotter mustard for adults, if preferred)
8 frankfurter sausages or wienerwurst (see box) or hot dogs
2 large onions, chopped
1 tbsp oil
1 tsp chili powder

1 Cut the rolls lengthwise, almost in half. Spread each roll with a teaspoonful of the mustard.

2 Cook the frankfurters according to the directions on the can or package, or, if fresh, drop into boiling water and simmer for about 5 minutes until heated through. Frankfurters can also be cooked in the microwave: place them on a plate and cook on High for about 1 minute.

3 Meanwhile, fry the onion in the oil in a heavy-based skillet for about 10 minutes or until softened and cooked. Sprinkle with the chili powder, mix well and cook for a further 2 minutes.

4 Spread equal amounts of the onion mixture into each roll.

5 Drain the frankfurters and add one to each roll.

6 Wrap the Hot Diggitty Dogs in paper napkins and serve immediately, while still piping hot.

DID YOU KNOW?

A long-standing rivalry exists between the *frankfurter* and the *wienerwurst*, both contenders for the title of original hot-dog sausage. The *frankfurter* from Germany and the Austrian *wienerwurst* are both lightly smoked. Traditionally they contain finely ground pork, but these days they may also contain beef.

Hot Diggitty Dogs taste delicious as they are but can be made extra special if you top with just a spoonful of barbecue sauce. A quick and easy one is made by mixing in a pan 1⅓ cups tomato ketchup, 2 tsp butter, ¼ tsp chili powder, 3 tbsp vinegar, 1 tsp brown sugar, ½ tsp chopped mixed herbs and salt and pepper to taste. Bring to a boil and simmer for 15 minutes. This is a delicious sauce to also serve with barbecued meat, fish and poultry.

STEP 1

STEP 2

STEP 4

STEP 5

WAGONS ROLL

Here is a very simple, if unusual, filled whole-wheat roll idea that is very popular with children. It is also very nutritious, and ideal to pop in a school lunch box.

SERVES 1

2 round whole-wheat rolls
2 tbsp butter or margarine
mustard
8 oz can baked beans in tomato sauce
1 tsp raisins
salt and pepper

VARIATIONS

Add a sprinkling of any of the following ingredients for a more "adult" version of this roll:

broiled bacon pieces
chopped mushrooms
chopped cooked ham
onion, chopped and fried

1 Cut the rolls in half and scoop out the soft bread from the top and bottom roll halves.

2 Make the soft bread that you have scooped out into crumbs by rubbing it against a coarse grater, then set it aside.

3 Spread the insides of the rolls with the butter or margarine and smear lightly with mustard to taste.

4 Mash the baked beans lightly with the scooped out and reserved bread crumbs, then add the raisins, and salt and pepper to taste. Mix in any additional ingredients you also wish to include in the roll.

5 Pile the filling back into the roll bases, replace the lids and wrap in foil for transporting.

THE WHOLE-WHEAT OPTION

Whole-wheat rolls add extra dietary fiber to this sandwich idea. Whole-wheat flour is made from the whole wheat grain which has been milled with nothing added or taken away. Stoneground whole-wheat flour is much the same, but it is made in the traditional way using grinding stones.

EGGS AHOY!

*These are miniature bread rolls that are perfect to serve at a children's party. They are fun to look at with their colorful and edible sails.
Set sail on a sea of chopped green lettuce!*

STEP 1

MAKES 12

12 small or miniature bread rolls
3 hard-boiled eggs, shelled
1½ tbsp mayonnaise
¼ cup butter or margarine
3 medium tomatoes
12 slices cucumber

1 Cut the tops off the bread rolls (forming a lid that will be used later) and scoop out some of the bread. Set the lids aside for the finishing touch.

2 Make bread crumbs from the scooped-out bread by rubbing it along a coarse grater, or by using a food processor. (A brief burst on high speed should be sufficient.)

3 Chop the hard-boiled eggs and mix with about half of the prepared crumbs (use the remainder for another dish). Stir in the mayonnaise to bind the mixture together.

4 Butter the rolls, then fill with the egg mixture and replace the tops.

5 Cut the tomatoes into quarters and remove the seeds. Place a slice of cucumber inside each tomato quarter.

6 Push a toothpick through each tomato quarter and cucumber slice, and use to represent a sail on each egg "boat". Serve as soon as possible to prevent the rolls from becoming soggy. If ripe tomatoes prove difficult to obtain, sails can also be made using a triangle of processed cheese.

STEP 2

STEP 3

PARTY CATERING

This is the perfect sandwich idea and the ideal opportunity to introduce mild herbs to children's food. Add 1-2 tsp chopped fresh parsley, chives or cilantro to the egg mixture to introduce new flavors in a familiar format.

Under-six-year-olds may be overwhelmed by the sheer excitement of a party so that their appetites disappear. Older children, however, will eat an astonishing amount – at least as much as adults. Be sure to have enough food on hand!

STEP 5

GAMEBOARD PIZZA SLICE

This is a super idea for a child's quickly assembled lunch. Use a thick slice of bread from an uncut loaf for best results.

STEP 2

STEP 3

STEP 4

STEP 5

SERVES 1

1 thick slice of bread
1 tbsp pizza sauce, or tomato paste
¼ cup Cheddar cheese, grated
1 slice cooked ham
1 small tomato
½ green bell pepper, cored

1 Lightly toast the bread until it is just lightly golden brown. (Overcooked bread will be too dry and won't "take" the flavors as well.)

2 Spread the slice of bread with the pizza sauce, or tomato paste.

3 Sprinkle the cheese on top to cover the slice evenly.

4 Cut the ham into long thin strips about ½-in wide and arrange on top of the cheese in a crisscross pattern to look like a zeros and crosses (tic-tac-toe) grid.

5 Slice the tomatoes to look like the zeros in a game, and slice the green bell pepper into thin strips so that two can be placed over each other to make

crosses. Arrange a few zeros and crosses over the cheesy grid. (With perhaps a winning sequence!)

6 Cook under a preheated hot broiler until hot and bubbly, about 3-4 minutes. Transfer to a heated plate to serve.

EASY PIZZA SAUCE

The supermarket is a ready source of pizza sauces, but if you are so inclined, a fresh sauce can be quickly created using the microwave. Drain and chop a can of tomatoes, then place in a bowl with a little garlic, oregano and salt and pepper. Cook on High for 2½ minutes, stirring once. The sauce will keep sealed in the refrigerator for a few days.

STEP 1

STEP 2

STEP 4

STEP 5

INITIAL ANSWERS

In this recipe slices of bread are topped with a tasty sardine or mackerel mixture, then topped with initials cut out from cheese slices. They make good party-time sandwiches for children.

MAKES 4

4 slices Cheddar cheese
4 oz canned sardines or mackerel, drained
2-in piece cucumber, very finely chopped
¼ small red bell pepper, cored, seeded and finely chopped, or 1 firm tomato, chopped
1 tbsp mayonnaise or plain yogurt
salt and pepper
4 small slices of white or whole-wheat bread

1 Using initial cutters or a sharp knife, cut 4 initials from the cheese slices to represent the first letter of the name of each of the diners. Gather together any cheese trimmings and chop them finely.

2 In a small bowl, use two forks to flake the sardines or mackerel and mix with the cucumber, red bell pepper or tomato, mayonnaise or yogurt, and salt and pepper to taste, mixing well. Add the reserved cheese trimmings and mix well.

3 Toast the bread until light golden brown.

4 Spread the slices of toast equally with the prepared sardine or mackerel mixture, spreading evenly to the edges of the bread.

5 Top each slice of bread with a cheese initial.

6 Serve as soon as possible, ideally with a knife and fork to make these open-faced sandwiches easy to eat.

INITIAL VARIATIONS

The initial idea can applied to other recipes, too. If you are cooking for non-fish eaters (particularly children), use cheese initials to top ham, tomato or pizza-style fillings.

The sandwich filling and cheesy topping described above also make a splendid topping for a pizza. For speed and convenience use a ready-prepared pizza base (about 9 inches in diameter). Top with 4-6 tbsp tomato sauce, spread with the prepared fish mixture, top with the cheese initials and bake in a hot oven for 12-15 minutes, until hot and bubbly.

STEP 3

STEP 4

STEP 5

STEP 6

CHEESE-AND-APPLE DELIGHT

It is important that children who take a sandwich lunch to school receive the same nourishment as those who eat a good cooked meal. This recipe is carefully balanced to provide many nutrients.

SERVES 1

2 country-style bread buns
¾ cup Cheddar cheese, grated coarsely
2 tbsp butter or margarine
1 green apple
2 pre-soaked dried apricots (optional)
1 tbsp plain yogurt
salt and pepper

1 Place the buns on a broiler tray and sprinkle with a small amount of the cheese. Place under a preheated hot broiler and cook until the cheese is just melted. Remove and allow to cool completely.

2 Split the buns in half and spread both pieces with the butter or margarine.

3 Core the apple but do not peel unless necessary. Coarsely grate the apple. In a bowl, combine the grated apple with the remaining cheese.

4 Snip the apricots, if using, into small pieces with kitchen scissors and add to the cheese filling, mixing well to combine.

5 Add the yogurt with salt and pepper to taste and mix well to blend.

6 Fill the buns with the cheese-and-apple mixture, pressing down gently to seal. Wrap tightly for transporting to school.

AN ENERGY LUNCH

This filled bun is the basis for a balanced children's lunch. Served with milk and a piece of fresh fruit, it provides an energy-packed and sustaining meal that will see your child through the afternoon.

Added interest, flavor and nutrition can be introduced to this recipe by using rolls that have seeded tops – such as cracked wheat, sesame seed, poppy seed, buckwheat or caraway seeds. Alternatively, sprinkle the rolls with a little grated cheese and grill until the cheese melts before filling with the cheese and apple mixture.

74

SANDWICH TECHNIQUES

Freezing Bread

Bread freezes extremely well, and it is always useful to have a few varieties stored away in the freezer. Keep all bread in heavy-duty plastic bags or foil and seal securely. Label and freeze for up to the following maximum times:

Crusty Breads	2 weeks
Rolls	2 weeks
Sliced Loaves	1 month
Uncut Loaves	2 months

Thaw bread, still in its wrapping, at room temperature. Large loaves may take as long as 4 hours to thaw, whereas rolls, French sticks and small braided loaves may take as little as 30 minutes. If you simply want to toast frozen sliced bread, do not bother to thaw it first – it will toast perfectly well from frozen.

Freshening Bread

Slightly stale bread can be freshened easily for same-day eating. Place the loaf or rolls in an ovenproof airtight cake container covered with foil or wrap completely in foil. Place in a hot oven (450°F) for 5-10 minutes. Cool the bread in the container. It is then ready for use. Slightly stale bread freshened this way will turn stale extremely quickly so must be used as soon as possible.

THE HISTORY OF THE SANDWICH

Legend says that in the first century of the Christian era the ancient Romans taught the early Britons how to make *offula* – that is, a combination of foods similar to what is now known to us as a sandwich. But when the Romans withdrew from England, the *offula* was soon forgotten, and was not rediscovered until the eighteenth century. It has not been forgotten since.

John Montague, fourth Earl of Sandwich, is generally credited with the invention of the sandwich. Seated at a gambling table and loath to leave it even for food, he called for slices of bread with beef between them to be brought to him so that he could continue playing with one hand while he ate his snack from the other.

It is unlikely that he was the first person to dream up this easy-to-eat, portable meal (the French say it had been peasant fare for centuries), but he probably made it acceptable. It would prove interesting to see the astonishment the lively Earl would display if he could see the development his invention has undergone since then.

THE BREAD

Bread is the major part of a sandwich, so make sure it is fresh. A new crusty loaf can be put in the refrigerator for a few hours to make it easier to slice. Ready-sliced bread is handy because you have a choice of thicknesses and the wrapping keeps it fresh longer.

To vary sandwiches use different types of bread. Some of the lighter rye breads are particularly delicious, especially those sprinkled with caraway seeds. Breads flavored with nuts, olives, sun-dried tomatoes and herbs make a welcome entrance when mixed and matched with suitable fillings.

Types of Bread

Bread has been made for at least 8,000 years, so it is not surprising that there are many varieties to choose from. Add to that the vast range of imported specialties and you can easily appreciate that the choices are wide and varied.

Whole-wheat breads These breads are made with less-refined flour than white loaves and have a slightly heavier texture and nuttier flavor. Some varieties also have nuts and seeds added for extra flavor, nutrition and interest.

White breads This is made from milled flour where most of the bran particles have been removed. Some bleaching of the flour also takes place to give the characteristic white appearance. The choices here are also wide, as all white flours are then enriched with vitamins by law, and paradoxically some have bran added back to the basic mixture.

Crusty loaves These loaves are mostly made with white flour (although increasingly more with whole-wheat, too) and open-baked on the floor of the oven to give a golden crusty casing.

Enriched loaves These breads are enriched in some way – by the addition of eggs and/or fat and/or milk –and include types of bread containing fruit and malt. They include fruit loaf; malt loaf (made with special malt meal, sometimes with added fruit); milk loaf; cholla (a version of the Jewish Ritriel Bread that is enriched with butter and eggs); and Vienna Bread (enriched with milk).

Proprietary breads These are white and whole-wheat breads made from special flours and recipes, and sold under brand names. They include bran loaves (available in both whole-wheat and white varieties); whole-wheat breads (some have added wheat germ or malted meal, while others are made from branded flours); and soda bread (baking soda is used as a raising agent instead of yeast, and the bread is usually cut into quarters from a large, flat loaf).

Pan loaves This category covers all types of bread baked in pans or containers. The description refers to the shape of the loaf; many can be made with either whole-wheat or white flours.

Rolls and Buns

In just the same way as there are dozens of varieties of loaves, there are just as many varieties of rolls and buns. Some of the most popular include whole-wheat, crusty white, fruited, rich such as brioche and croissants and soft white and wholemeal.

European varieties

The last few years have seen a veritable explosion of interest in different breads, and supermarkets have responded by stocking a wide range of specialties from home and abroad. Local bakers have resurrected many breads that were popular years ago and have also produced some new bread ideas. You may find Italian ciabatta and olive-studded foccacia bread alongside French brioche and baguettes, or cornbread and muffins rubbing shoulders with bagels, and homemade specialty marbled breads swirled with onions, cheese, herbs, sun-dried tomatoes and pesto sauce.

With such variety no one should lack inspiration for creating a super sandwich!

BUTTERING

A sandwich should be really mouth-watering, both in appearance and flavor, no matter if it is just a bite or a meal in itself. This means that every stage of sandwich making should be carefully considered – especially the buttering.

Do not skimp on the butter or margarine – spread it right to the very edges of the bread or sandwich because the butter or margarine adds flavor, helps to hold the filling ingredients together and acts as a waterproof coat and prevents fillings from soaking through and making the bread soggy.

Alternatives to Butter

For variety experiment with sweet butter and using other interesting

Storing Bread

Keeping bread fresh depends upon several factors. Sliced, white bread, enriched doughs and slimmers' breads will keep fresh for several days, but loaves such as Vienna or French should almost always be used immediately. Other factors which affect storage include the length of time the bread was baked and storage conditions.

- Ideally bread should be stored in a clean container. Wash out bread bins with hot soapy water every week. This discourages mold from growing.

- Keep bread in a dry container at normal room temperature, making sure that the container allows the circulation of air.

- Keep any wrapped bread stored in its wrapper. Any uncut loaves can be stored in a plastic bag but not tied so securely that air cannot circulate.

- Contrary to popular belief, bread "stales" more quickly in the refrigerator than at normal room temperature, so do not store it in the refrigerator.

Flavored Butters
Flavored butters add interest and perk up traditional fillings, so make up a batch of them and store in the refrigerator for up to 2 weeks.

Mustard Butter Cream ¼ cup butter or margarine until soft, then gradually beat in 1 teaspoon English or 2 teaspoons French mustard. Use in sandwiches containing beef, lamb, bacon, ham, shellfish, herring or mackerel.

Horseradish Butter Cream ¼ cup butter or margarine until soft, then gradually beat in 2 teaspoons grated fresh horseradish or 1-2 teaspoons creamed horseradish sauce. If using ready-prepared horseradish check the strength of your brand because they differ widely from mild to very hot. Use in sandwiches containing beef, herring, mackerel or smoked trout.

Lemon Butter Cream ¼ cup butter or margarine until soft, then gradually beat in 1 teaspoon finely grated lemon rind and 1 teaspoon lemon juice. Use in sandwiches containing fish, veal or chicken.

spreads such as mayonnaise, meat, fish, game and other savory spreads, bouillon-based spreads, peanut butter and well-seasoned vegetable or fruit spreads. You may find these more unusual spreads in health-food stores.

THE FILLING
Always fill sandwiches generously and do not forget the seasonings. Fillings should be more highly seasoned than the same ingredients without bread. If a smooth filling is used such as cream cheese, leave it at room temperature for about 15 minutes – it will then be easier to spread.

Remember, too, that diffferent tastes are obtained by spreading each filling separately. For instance, if you are using peanut butter and jelly, the two flavors will be more pronounced if the peanut butter is spread on one slice of bread and the jelly on the other than if the two were blended and spread on both sides.

There is a host of sandwich ideas in the recipes in this book, but for added inspiration, try some of the following additional ideas:

Banana Mash with lemon juice and light cream. Add shredded coconut or tiny crispy fried pieces of bacon.

Beef Cut into very thin slices and use on bread spread with horseradish sauce or mustard. Add coleslaw, sliced gherkins or cucumber.

Blue cheese Spread on whole-wheat or mixed-grain bread. Add crisp romain lettuce, thin slices of apple or grated carrot.

Cheese Slice or grate hard types. Add pickle, mustard, sliced raw onions, tomato, ham, pineapple, chopped celery in mayonnaise, shredded lettuce or sliced cucumber.

Chicken or turkey These are best if they are finely chopped and mixed with mayonnaise, sour cream, yogurt or natural fromage frais. Add slivered almonds, scallions, pineapple chunks, golden raisins, crisp lettuce or mustard.

Corned beef Slice or break up by mashing. Add horseradish relish, chopped gherkins or capers in mayonnaise, tomatoes, coleslaw, parsley or chive-flavored butter.

Cream cheese Spread onto bread or mix with flavorings first. Add chives, scallions, dates, raisins, golden raisins, celery, apple, walnuts, diced cucumber, shrimp or smoked salmon, crispy fried bacon pieces or capers.

Egg Hard-boil and slice, or mash with a little milk, or scramble. Add chopped gherkins, bell peppers, diced shrimp or smoked salmon, chives, parsley, curry powder, onion salt and cucumber.

Lamb Trim away any fat from thin slices. Add tomato, gherkins, mint jelly, coleslaw, orange-flavored mayonnaise, shredded lettuce or sliced cucumber.

Liver sausage Slice finely or spread. Add grated carrot, coleslaw, fine slices of raw onion or apple, gherkins or tomato.

Pork Dice or slice finely. Add shredded lettuce, tomato, applesauce, a relish, chutney or pineapple in a thick mayonnaise.

Shrimp and crab Shell and chop. Add cream cheese, chives in mayonnaise, sliced avocado tossed in lemon juice, crisp lettuce or anchovy-flavored butter.

Sardines, tuna or mackerel Drain and mash. Add lemon-flavored mayonnaise, tomatoes, crisp cucumber, lettuce or celery salt.

Salami, ham or luncheon meat Slice thinly and add pickles, chutney, coleslaw, tomatoes, lettuce or cucumber.

THE GARNISH

Suitable garnishes or decorations for sandwiches add good looks as well as flavor – but they must be as fresh as the bread, the butter and the filling. Colors should be chosen to tone with both the food and its setting or serving dish, and the flavor should complement the sandwich base and the filling or topping.

Use carrot curls and gherkin fans, which always stay fresh and suit both hot and cold sandwiches; radish roses or water lilies, which are most attractive on open sandwiches; celery curls and scallion curls can add a dash of sophistication to the plainest of sandwich fare; citrus twists, lemon butterflies and cucumber pinwheels give color and flavor to fish and shellfish; and pepper and beet shapes – but add these at the last minute just before serving to prevent "bleeding".

FOOD ON THE MOVE

Sandwiches make the perfect food for packed lunches for the office, factory or school – and, of course, they feature in alfresco meals.

For first-class results try to make sure that the packed lunch is as varied as possible. Combine different sandwiches in the same lunch box – easy if you have made a batch in bulk well ahead and frozen them. Remember to freeze only those sandwiches with fillings that freeze well, so forget tomato and lettuce, egg and avocado offerings. Alternate crisp rolls and fillings with soft breads and smoother fillings, and sweet with savory combinations. Remember to choose fillings that are not too wet.

Packed sandwiches can spell delight or disaster depending upon how they are prepared and packed. Rigid containers will ensure that the sandwiches arrive in one firm, whole piece rather than squashed. Foil, waxed paper and plastic wrap will stop any transference of flavor from one sandwich to another.

Finally, add a napkin – sandwiches may seem perfect in every way for the lunch box, but they can still produce sticky fingers!

Herb Butters

Herb butters will prove infinitely useful for adding to broiled meats, fish, game or poultry, cooked vegetables and, of course, for making sandwiches.

Green Goddess Butter Cream ¼ cup butter or margarine until soft, then gradually beat in 1 teaspoon each of finely chopped tarragon, chervil and parsley, 2 finely chopped baby spinach leaves and 1 teaspoon finely grated onion. Use in sandwiches containing fish.

Watercress Butter Trim and wash 1 bunch watercress, then blend or pound into a smooth paste with a mortar and pestle or food processor. Cream ¼ cup butter or margarine until soft, then gradually beat in the watercress paste, a pinch of sugar, and salt and pepper to taste. Pass through a fine strainer if liked and use in sandwiches containing meat or fish.

Garlic Butter Cream ¼ cup butter or margarine until soft, then gradually beat in 2 peeled and crushed cloves of garlic. Use in sandwiches containing steak and robust-flavored vegetables.

Chive Butter Cream ¼ cup butter or margarine until soft, then gradually beat in 2 teaspoons finely snipped chives and 1 teaspoon lemon juice. Use in sandwiches containing chicken, vegetables or meat.

INDEX